Creepy Crawly Things

Reptiles and Amphibians

BOOKS FOR YOUNG EXPLORERS
NATIONAL GEOGRAPHIC SOCIETY

TOKAY GECKO, EASTERN ASIA

Snakes are strange
and beautiful creatures.
These snakes are cobras.
They are very poisonous.
But most snakes are harmless
and cannot hurt you.

The gecko with big round eyes
is a harmless lizard.
It can race up a wall
and even across a ceiling.

Lizards and snakes are reptiles.
Reptiles have bodies
covered with small, hard scales.
Alligators, crocodiles, and turtles
are reptiles too.

COBRA, INDIA AND AFRICA

A newt is a salamander
that lives most of its life
in the water.
A newt hatches from eggs
laid in wet places,
just like other salamanders.
Newts and salamanders then
leave the water to live on land.
But after a while,
the newt goes back to the water.

A tiny frog sits
on the tip of a man's finger.
A frog usually starts its life
in the water.
Then it lives mostly on land.

Frogs, toads, and salamanders
are amphibians.
Amphibians spend part of
their lives in water
and part on land.

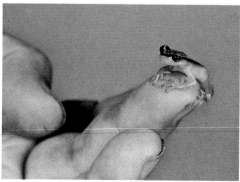

TRINIDAD TREE FROG

ALPINE NEWT, EUROPE

A newt peeps over
a plant in a pond.
Can you see the newt
reflected in the water?

Most salamanders live on land in cool, moist places.
They hide under rocks, logs, or piles of leaves.
They come out at night or on rainy days to hunt for insects and worms.
Perhaps there is a salamander hiding near your house.

7

A baby salamander has gills
near its head.
They look like little feathers.
The gills let the salamander
breathe underwater, just as fishes do.
As salamanders grow up,
most of them lose their gills.
They climb out of the water.
Then they breathe air with lungs,
just as people do.
Some live in damp woodlands
where mushrooms grow.

FIRE SALAMANDER, LARVAL STAGE

FIRE SALAMANDER, EUROPE

STRAWBERRY FROG, PANAMA AND COSTA RICA

FOWLER'S TOAD, EASTERN U. S.

GREEN TREE FROG, SOUTHEASTERN U. S.

Frogs have smooth, wet skin.
Toads have skin that is dry and bumpy.

A tree frog has round pads
on the tips of its toes. The pads help it
climb a tree or hold onto a twig.

Frogs have strong hind legs
and are very good jumpers.
Toads are fatter than frogs.
They cannot jump as well as frogs.
They just hop, hop, hop along.

FOWLER'S TOAD

In the springtime a male toad hops
to the nearest pond and begins to sing.
His throat puffs out like a balloon.
He sings a song to call a female toad.
Soon the female comes to the pond
and mates with the male.

The female toad lays a long string of eggs
in the water. The eggs look like black beads.
Clear jelly covers the eggs and protects them.

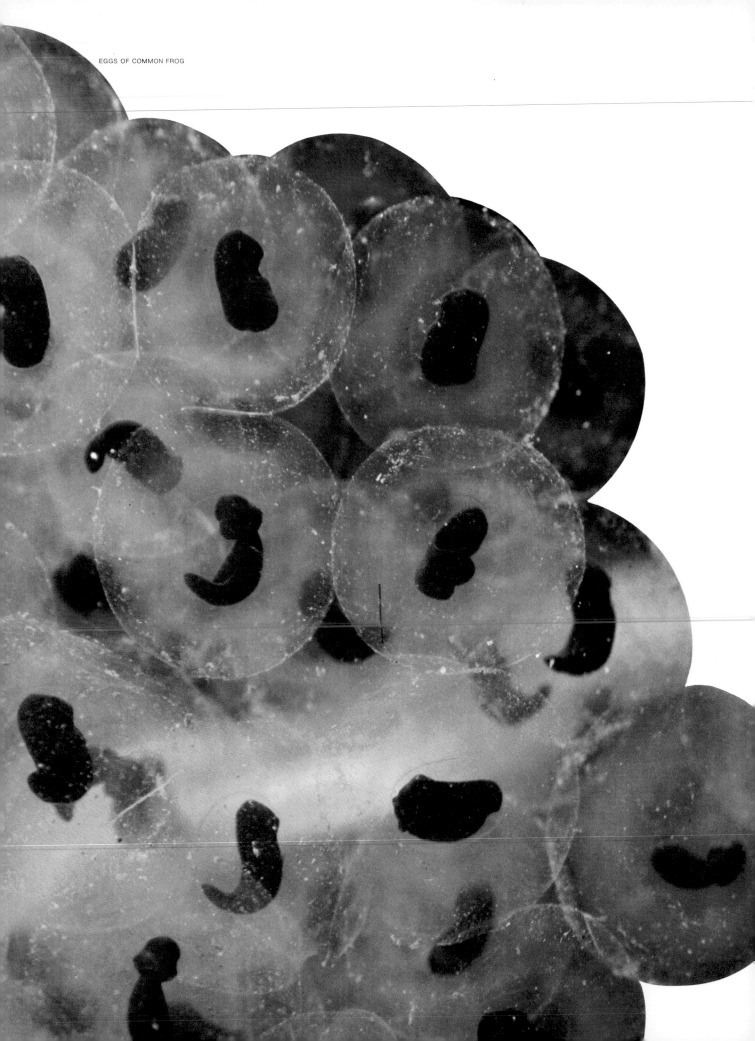

Frogs lay their eggs in the water too.
These eggs are in bunches like grapes.
After a few days, there is a tadpole
in the middle of each round egg.
The tadpole has gills and a tail.
When the egg hatches,
the tadpole wiggles around in the water.
Do you live near a pond or creek?
If you look carefully,
you may find tadpoles there.

COMMON FROG, EUROPE (TOP); COMMON FROG, NEWLY HATCHED TADPOLES

PACIFIC TREE FROG, TADPOLE

As the tadpole gets bigger,
skin grows over the gills.
The hind legs grow first.
Then the front legs grow too.
Its long tail gets shorter
and shorter.
Soon the tadpole
will have no tail at all.
Then it will be
a frog!

PACIFIC TREE FROG, WEST COAST U. S.
(ABOVE AND LEFT)

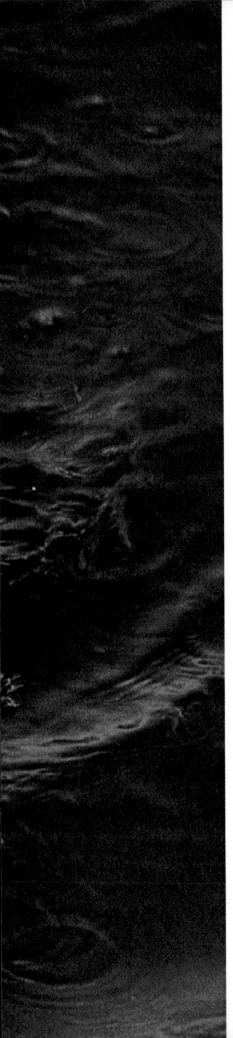

Alligators catch fish in their big jaws.
These reptiles spend most of their lives in the water.
The mother alligator leaves the water to lay her eggs.
She builds a big nest of plants and mud.
Then she lays her eggs in the nest
and stays nearby until they hatch.

All turtles hatch from eggs. As soon as sea turtles hatch,
they hurry down the beach to their home in the sea.
Sea turtles hardly ever leave the water again. But the mother turtle
comes out of the water to lay her eggs on the beach.
Then the mother turtle slowly crawls back to the sea.

COLLARED LIZARD, SOUTH CENTRAL U. S.

Many lizards have long tails.
If an enemy grabs one of these lizards, the tail snaps off.
Then the lizard runs away. Later it grows a new tail.
The flying lizard spreads flaps of skin that look like wings.
When this lizard jumps from tree to tree, it glides through the air.
The green tree lizard has long thin toes that help it to climb branches.
The Gila monster is a lizard too.
It is the only poisonous lizard in the United States.

FLYING LIZARD, SOUTHEAST ASIA (TOP); GREEN TREE LIZARD, GUATEMALA AND SOUTHERN MEXICO

GILA MONSTER, SOUTHWESTERN U. S. AND NORTHERN MEXICO

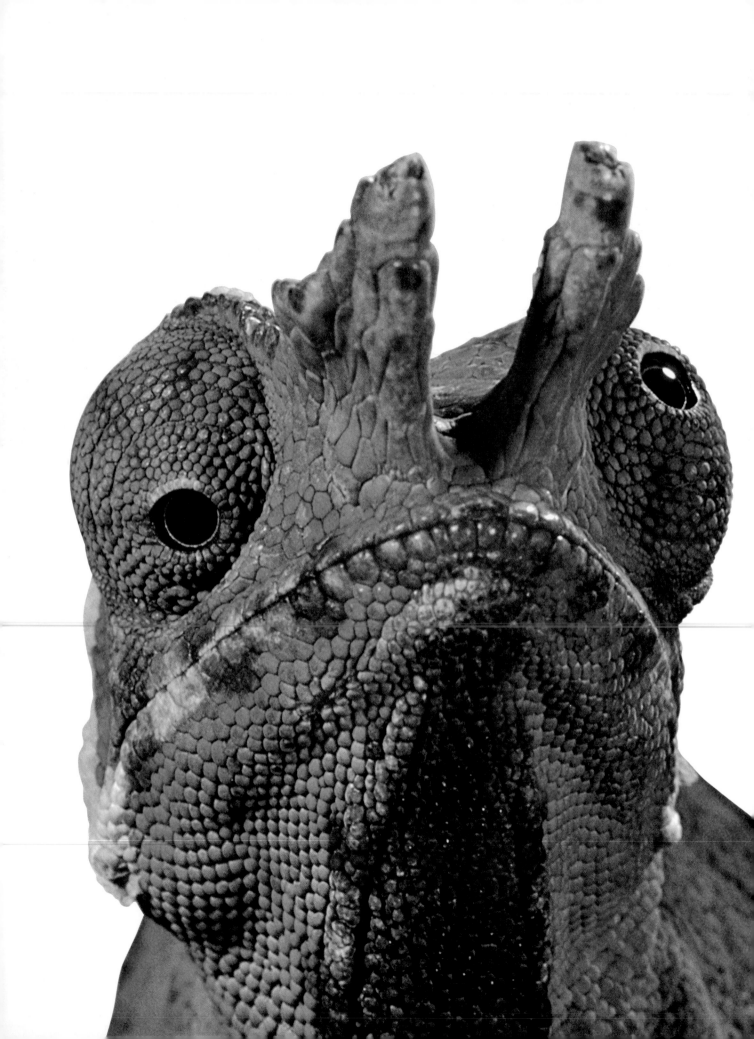

African chameleons are lizards that can change their colors.
Some chameleons have horns and look like little dinosaurs.
Skin covers their big popeyes, but they can see through peepholes.
Each eye moves by itself. One eye can look to the front
while the other eye rolls around to look to the side or back.

A chameleon has a very long tongue.
It may be longer than the whole body.
When an insect comes near, the chameleon shoots out
its tongue. It has a sticky pad at the tip.
The insect sticks to the tip. And before you can say "chameleon,"
the insect is eaten up.

The marine iguana creeps
along the bottom of the sea.
This lizard dives
for seaweeds to eat.
These iguanas sun themselves
on the rocky beaches
where they live.

The Komodo dragon is
the world's largest lizard.
A big one is longer than your bed.
This giant lizard uses its claws
to hold wild pigs
and other animals it eats.

KOMODO DRAGON, SUNDA ISLANDS, INDONESIA

MARINE IGUANA, GALAPAGOS ISLANDS (LEFT AND ABOVE)

RAINBOW BOA,
SOUTH AND CENTRAL AMERICA

RIBBON SNAKE, EASTERN U. S.

Some snakes have scales in bright colors
and are easy to see. Others are hard to see
because they match the ground or trees where they live.
As snakes grow, they get too big for their skins. The skin doesn't stretch.
So the snake wiggles out of its old skin and leaves it behind.

COTTONMOUTH MOCCASIN, SOUTHEASTERN U. S. (TOP); TIMBER RATTLESNAKE, EASTERN U. S.

A snake uses its tongue to help it smell.
When the tongue moves in and out,
the snake can tell
if other animals are near.

A rattlesnake has rattles
on the end of its tail.
It shakes the rattles
to warn enemies to keep away.

TREE VIPER, SOUTHERN MEXICO AND CENTRAL AMERICA

The snakes on these two pages
are very poisonous.
Only poisonous snakes have fangs.
The fangs are sharp, hollow teeth.
When the snake bites, the fangs fill with poison.
The poison kills mice, lizards, and frogs,
and the other small animals a snake eats.
The poison can kill people too.

CORAL SNAKE. SOUTHEASTERN U. S.

Most snakes are not poisonous.
When the red and yellow corn snake catches its dinner,
it will coil around the animal and squeeze it to death.

Many snakes help farmers
by catching rats and mice that eat crops.
The rough green snake helps farmers by eating insects.
Even the tiny red-bellied snake helps man by eating insects.

Reptiles and amphibians can be as small as a pencil.
Others are very large.
These creepy crawly things can be strange,
and they can be very beautiful.
They are all part of the world of nature.

ROUGH GREEN SNAKE, SOUTHERN AND CENTRAL U. S.

RED-BELLIED SNAKE, EASTERN U. S.

CORN SNAKE, SOUTHEASTERN U. S.

SOUTH AMERICAN HORNED FROG

Published by The National Geographic Society
Melvin M. Payne, *President;* Melville Bell Grosvenor, *Editor-in-Chief;*
Gilbert M. Grosvenor, *Editor.*

Prepared by
The Special Publications Division
Robert L. Breeden, *Editor*
Donald J. Crump, *Associate Editor*
Philip B. Silcott, *Senior Editor*
Robert M. McClung, *Consulting Editor*
Cynthia Russ Ramsay, *Managing Editor*
Harriet H. Watkins, *Research*

Illustrations, Design and Art Direction
Geraldine Linder, *Picture Editor*
Joseph A. Taney, *Staff Art Director*
Josephine B. Bolt, *Associate Art Director*
Ursula Perrin, *Staff Designer*

Production and Printing
Robert W. Messer, *Production Manager*
George V. White, *Assistant Production Manager*
Raja D. Murshed, Nancy W. Glaser, *Production Assistants*
John R. Metcalfe, *Engraving and Printing*
Mary G. Burns, Jane H. Buxton, Marta Isabel Coons, Suzanne J. Jacobson,
   Joan Perry, Marilyn L. Wilbur, *Staff Assistants*

Consultants
Dr. Glenn O. Blough, *Educational Consultant*
Department of Reptiles and Amphibians, Smithsonian Institution,
   Washington, D. C., Scientific Consultants
Edith K. Chasnov, Lynn Z. Lang, *Reading Specialists*

Illustrations Credits

James H. Carmichael, Jr. *(endsheets, 2, 10 bottom left and right, 29, 31 top left);* Paul A. Zahl,
National Geographic Staff (1, 10-11); James P. Blair, *National Geographic Photographer (2-3);*
Robert C. Hermes *(4);* Jane Burton, *Bruce Coleman Inc. (4-5, 6, 8 left, 8-9, 12-13, 14, 15 top and
bottom left);* Alan Blank, *Bruce Coleman Inc. (6-7, 15 top, center, and bottom right, 23, 26);*
Robert S. Simmons *(13, 21 top and bottom, 26-27, 28-29);* Winfield Parks, *National Geographic
Photographer (16-17);* Joe Van Wormer, *Bruce Coleman Inc. (17 top);* Treat Davidson *(17 bottom);*
Robert E. Schroeder *(18 all, 18-19);* David G. Allen *(20-21);* Bates Littlehales, *National
Geographic Photographer (21 center);* Constance Warner *(22, 32);* Edmund S. Hobson *(24 top);*
Kenneth W. Fink, *Bruce Coleman Inc. (24-25);* David S. Boyer, *National Geographic Staff
(25 top);* James H. Robinson *(28 top, 30-31, 31 top right);* R. Allan Winstrel, *National
Audubon Society (28 bottom).*   Cover Photograph: Jane Burton, *Bruce Coleman Inc.*